Piano • Vocal • Guitar

MW00489129

# Love Songs of the 70's

ISBN 0-7935-4591-9

HAL•LEONARD™
CORPORATION

7777 W. BLUEMOUND RD. P.O. BOX 13819 MILWAUKEE, WI 53213

# AFTER THE LOVE HAS GONE

Words and Music by DAVID FOSTER,
JAY GRAYDON and BILL CHAMPLIN

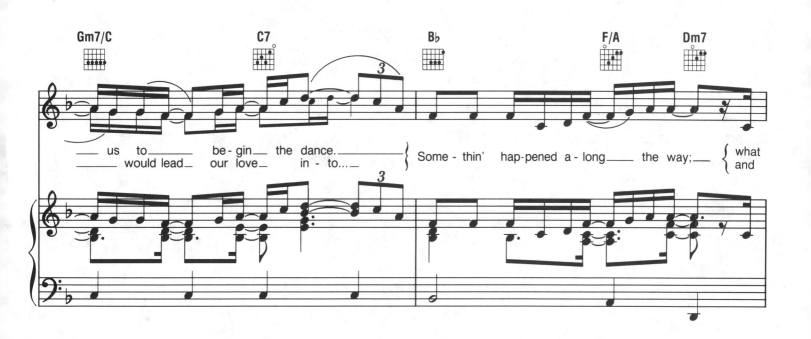

# AND I LOVE YOU SO

Words and Music by
DON McLEAN

# ANNIE'S SONG

Words and Music by
JOHN DENVER

# BEST THING THAT EVER HAPPENED TO ME

Words and Music by
JIM WEATHERLY

# BABY, I'M-A WANT YOU

Words and Music by
DAVID GATES

Used to be my life was just __ e-mo-tions pass-ing __ by, ___

feel-ing all the while and nev - er real - ly know-ing __ why. __

Late-ly, I'm a-pray-in'          that you'll al - ways be __ a-stay - in' ___ be - side __

# COME MONDAY

Words and Music by
JIMMY BUFFETT

# CAN'T SMILE WITHOUT YOU

Words and Music by CHRIS ARNOLD,
DAVID MARTIN and GEOFF MORROW

# (THEY LONG TO BE)
# CLOSE TO YOU

Words by HAL DAVID
Music by BURT BACHARACH

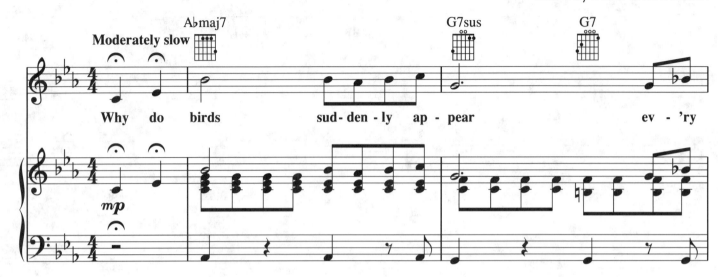

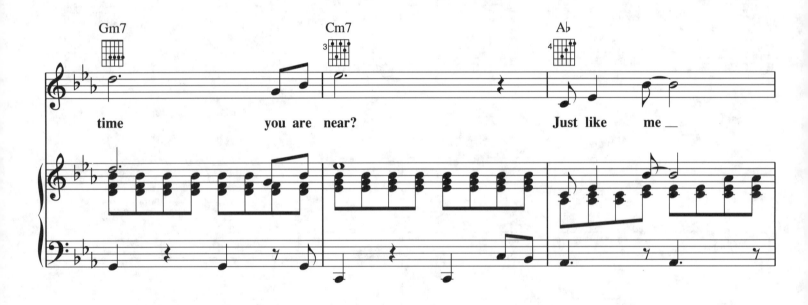

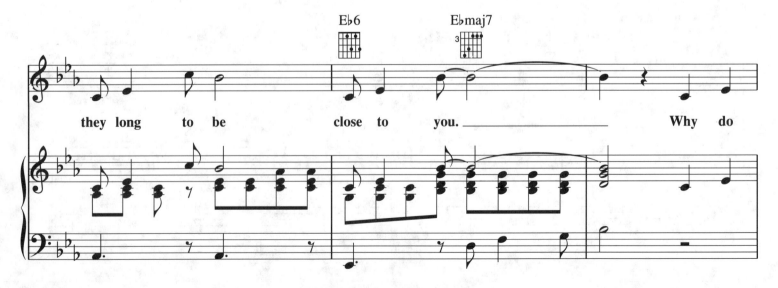

# THE CLOSER I GET TO YOU

Words and Music by JAMES MTUME
and REGGIE LUCAS

# DEJA VU

Lyrics by ADRIENNE ANDERSON
Music by ISAAC HAYES

## Additional Verses:

*Verse 3*  This is divine; I've been waiting all my life, filling time.
Looking for you, nights were more than you could know, long ago.

*Verse 4*  Come to me now; we don't have to dream of love, we know how.
Somewhere before it's as if I loved you so long ago. *(To Chorus:)*

# DIARY

Words and Music by
DAVID GATES

Moderately

**Gmaj7**    **Gmaj7sus**    **C/G**    **G**

*mp*

**Gmaj7**    **F/G**    **C6/G**

I found her dia - ry un - der-neath the tree, __ and start-ed read - ing a-bout
Then she con-front - ed with the writ - ing there, __ sim - ply pre-tend-ing not to care. __
I found her dia - ry un - der-neath the tree, __ and start-ed read - ing a-bout

**G**    **Gmaj7**    **F/G**

__ me. The words __ she'd writ-ten took me by __ sur-prise. __
__ me. I passed __ it off as just in keep - ing with __
__ me. The words __ be - gin to stick then tears __ to fall. __

**C6/G**    **G**    **Edim7**

You'd nev - er read __ them in her eyes. __ They said that
her to - tal dis - con-cert-ing air. __ And tho' she
Her mean-ing now __ was clear to see. __ The love she'd

# FEELINGS
## (¿DIME?)

English Words and Music by MORRIS ALBERT
Spanish lyric by THOMAS FUNDORA

# THE FIRST TIME EVER I SAW YOUR FACE

Words and Music by
EWAN MacCOLL

# FOR ALL WE KNOW

### from the Motion Picture LOVERS AND OTHER STRANGERS

Words by ROBB WILSON and JAMES GRIFFIN
Music by FRED KARLIN

Moderato, with a light beat

Love,_____ look at the two of us,_____ Stran-gers _____ in man-y ways.

54

# HELLO, IT'S ME

Words and Music by
TODD RUNDGREN

You know that I'd be with you if I could___ I'll come a-round to see you

once in a while___ or if I ev-er need a rea-son to smile___

And spend the night___ if you think I should.___

*To Coda*

Some-times I thought it was-n't so bad.___

*D. S. al Coda*

*Coda*

**Repeat and Fade**

# HOPELESSLY DEVOTED TO YOU
## from GREASE

Words and Music by
JOHN FARRAR

Moderate 2

Guess mine is not the first_____ heart bro - ken,
know I'm just a fool_____ who's will - in'_____
head is say - in', "Fool,_____ for - get him."

My
to
My

eyes are not the first_____ to cry.
sit a - round and wait_____ for you.
heart is say - in', "Don't_____ let go.

I'm
But,

# HOW DEEP IS YOUR LOVE

from the Motion Picture SATURDAY NIGHT FEVER

Words and Music by BARRY GIBB,
MAURICE GIBB and ROBIN GIBB

# IF

Words and Music by
DAVID GATES

# JUST THE WAY YOU ARE

Words and Music by
BILLY JOEL

Don't go chang-ing ___ to try and please me ___ You nev-er

let me down be-fore ___ mm ___ mm ___ don't im-ag - ine ___

# THE LAST TIME I FELT LIKE THIS

from SAME TIME, NEXT YEAR

Words by ALAN BERGMAN and MARILYN BERGMAN
Music by MARVIN HAMLISCH

Hel - lo, I don't_ e - ven know_ your name, but I'm hop - in' all_ the
lo, I can't_ wait till we're_ a - lone, some-where qui - et on_ our

same this is more than just a sim - ple hel - lo. Hel - I
own so that we can just fall the rest of the way.

MCA music publishing

# THE LONG AND WINDING ROAD

Words and Music by JOHN LENNON
and PAUL McCARTNEY

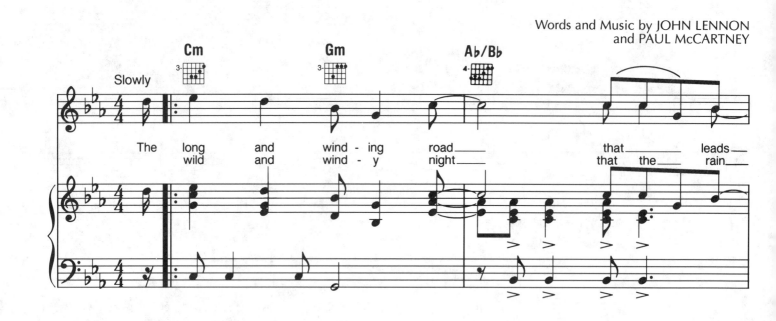

The long and wind-ing road_____ that_____ the leads
wild and and wind-y night_____ that the_____ leads rain_____

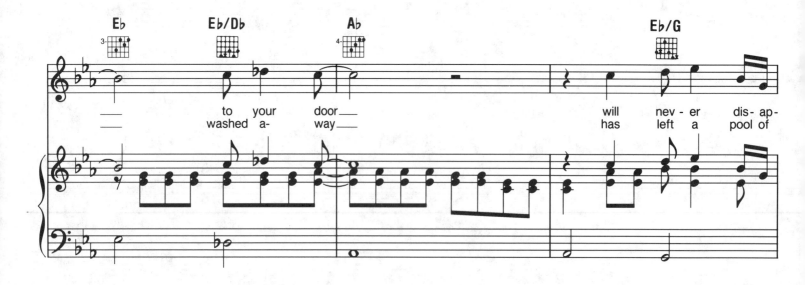

_____ to your door_____ will nev-er dis-ap-
_____ washed a-way_____ has left a pool of

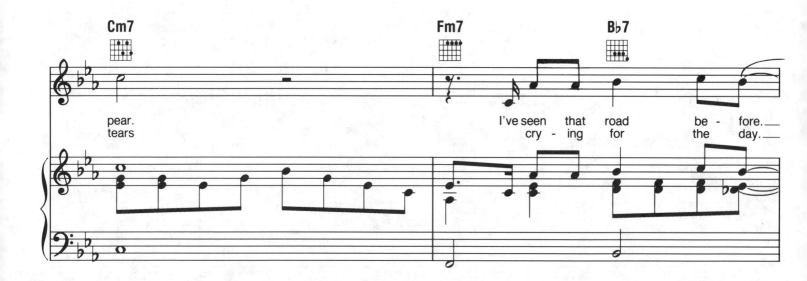

pear. I've seen that road be- fore._____
tears cry-ing for the day.

# LONGER

Words and Music by
DAN FOGELBERG

Long - er than__ there've been fish - es in the o - cean,
Strong - er than__ an - y moun - tain cath - e - dral.
Through the years__ as the fi - re starts to mel - low,

84

# MAKE IT WITH YOU

Words and Music by
DAVID GATES

# MY SWEET LADY

Words and Music by
JOHN DENVER

# PLEASE COME TO BOSTON

Words and Music by
DAVE LOGGINS

**ADDITIONAL LYRICS**

Verse 3.
    Please come to L.A. to live forever
    A California life alone is just too hard to build
    I live in a house that looks out over the ocean
    And there's some stars that fell from the sky
    Living up on the hill
    Please come to L.A., she just said no,
    Boy, won't you come home to me.
Repeat Chorus

# PRECIOUS AND FEW

Words and Music by
WALTER D. NIMS

# READY TO TAKE A CHANCE AGAIN
## (LOVE THEME)
### from the Paramount Picture FOUL PLAY

Words by NORMAN GIMBEL
Music by CHARLES FOX

# RIGHT TIME OF THE NIGHT

Words and Music by
PETER McCANN

# SHE BELIEVES IN ME

Words and Music by
STEVE GIBB

# SHE'S ALWAYS A WOMAN

Words and Music by
BILLY JOEL

D. S. al Coda

Coda

most she will do is throw sha-dows at you But she's al-ways a wom-an to

me. _____ (Hum) _____ (Hum) _____

rit.

# SOMETIMES WHEN WE TOUCH

Words by DAN HILL
Music by BARRY MANN

ask me if___ I love___ you,___ and I choke on my___ re-ply.___
mance and all___ its strat - e - gy leaves me bat - tling with___ my pride.___
times I un - der-stand___ you, and I know how hard___ you've tried.___

123

# SO FAR AWAY

Words and Music by
CAROLE KING

# SPEAK SOFTLY, LOVE
### (LOVE THEME)

from the Paramount Picture THE GODFATHER

Words by LARRY KUSIK
Music by NINO ROTA

# WHAT A DIFFERENCE YOU'VE MADE IN MY LIFE

Words and Music by
ARCHIE JORDAN

# WHERE DO I BEGIN
## (LOVE THEME)
### from the Paramount Picture LOVE STORY

Words by CARL SIGMAN
Music by FRANCIS LAI

**Slowly**

*With pedal*

Where do I be-gin _____ to tell the sto-ry of how
With her first hel-lo _____ she gave a mean-ing to this

great a love can be, _____ the sweet love sto-ry that is
emp-ty world of mine. _____ There'd nev-er be an-oth-er

old-er than the sea, the sim-ple truth a-bout the
love, an-oth-er time; she came in-to my life and

# WHEN I NEED YOU

Words by CAROLE BAYER SAGER
Music by ALBERT HAMMOND

Moderately, with feeling

When I Need You, I just close my eyes and I'm with you, and all that I saw, want ___ to give you, It's on-ly a heart-beat_ a way. ___

# YOU DECORATED MY LIFE

Words and Music by DEBBIE HUPP
and BOB MORRISON

# YOU NEEDED ME

Words and Music by
RANDY GOODRUM

Moderately

I cried a tear, you wiped it dry, I was con- fused you cleared my
hand, when it was cold, when I was lost you took me

mind, I sold my soul, you bought it back for me___ and held me
home You gave me hope, when I was at the end___ and turned my

# YOU'VE GOT A FRIEND

Words and Music by
CAROLE KING

# YOUR SONG

Words and Music by ELTON JOHN
and BERNIE TAUPIN

# Contemporary Classics

## Your favorite songs for piano, voice and guitar.

### The Definitive Rock 'n' Roll Collection

A classic collection of the best songs from the early rock 'n' roll years – 1955-1966. 97 songs, including: Barbara Ann • Chantilly Lace • Dream Lover • Duke Of Earl • Earth Angel • Great Balls Of Fire • Louie, Louie • Rock Around The Clock • Ruby Baby • Runaway • (Seven Little Girls) Sitting In The Back Seat • Stay • Surfin' U.S.A. • Wild Thing • Woolly Bully • and more.

00490195 ............................................$24.95

### The Big Book Of Rock

78 of rock's biggest hits, including: Addicted To Love • American Pie • Born To Be Wild • Cold As Ice • Dust In The Wind • Free Bird • Goodbye Yellow Brick Road • Groovin' • Hey Jude • I Love Rock N Roll • Lay Down Sally • Layla • Livin' On A Prayer • Louie Louie • Maggie May • Me And Bobby McGee • Monday, Monday • Owner Of A Lonely Heart • Shout • Walk This Way • We Didn't Start The Fire • You Really Got Me • and more.

00311566 ............................................$19.95

### Big Book Of Movie And TV Themes

Over 90 familiar themes, including: Alfred Hitchcock Theme • Beauty And The Beast • Candle On The Water • Theme From *E.T.* • Endless Love • Hawaii Five-O • I Love Lucy • Theme From *Jaws* • Jetsons • Major Dad Theme • The Masterpiece • Mickey Mouse March • The Munsters Theme • Theme From *Murder, She Wrote* • Mystery • Somewhere Out There • Unchained Melody • Won't You Be My Neighbor • and more!

00311582 ............................................$19.95

### The Best Rock Songs Ever

70 of the best rock songs from yesterday and today, including: All Day And All Of The Night • All Shook Up • Ballroom Blitz • Bennie And The Jets • Blue Suede Shoes • Born To Be Wild • Boys Are Back In Town • Every Breath You Take • Faith • Free Bird • Hey Jude • I Still Haven't Found What I'm Looking For • Livin' On A Prayer • Lola • Louie Louie • Maggie May • Money • (She's) Some Kind Of Wonderful • Takin' Care Of Business • Walk This Way • We Didn't Start The Fire • We Got The Beat • Wild Thing • more!

00490424 ...............................................$16.95

### The Best Of 90s Rock

30 songs, including: Alive • I'd Do Anything For Love (But I Won't Do That) • Livin' On The Edge • Losing My Religion • Two Princes • Walking On Broken Glass • Wind Of Change • and more.

00311668 ...............................................$14.95

### 35 Classic Hits

35 contemporary favorites, including: Beauty And The Beast • Dust In The Wind • Just The Way You Are • Moon River • The River Of Dreams • Somewhere Out There • Tears In Heaven • When I Fall In Love • A Whole New World (Aladdin's Theme) • and more.

00311654 ............................................$12.95

### 55 Contemporary Standards

55 favorites, including: Alfie • Beauty And The Beast • Can't Help Falling In Love • Candle In The Wind • Have I Told You Lately • How Am I Supposed To Live Without You • Memory • The River Of Dreams • Sea Of Love • Tears In Heaven • Up Where We Belong • When I Fall In Love • and more.

00311670 ............................................$15.95

### The New Grammy® Awards Song Of The Year Songbook

Every song named Grammy Awards' "Song Of The Year" from 1958 to 1988. 28 songs, featuring: Volare • Moon River • The Shadow Of Your Smile • Up, Up and Away • Bridge Over Troubled Water • You've Got A Friend • Killing Me Softly With His Song • The Way We Were • You Light Up My Life • Evergreen • Sailing • Bette Davis Eyes • We Are The World • That's What Friends Are For • Somewhere Out There • Don't Worry, Be Happy.

00359932 ............................................$12.95

### Soft Rock – Revised

39 romantic mellow hits, including: Beauty And The Beast • Don't Know Much • Save The Best For Last • Vision Of Love • Just Once • Dust In The Wind • Just The Way You Are • Your Song.

00311596 ............................................$14.95

### 37 Super Hits Of The Superstars

37 big hits by today's most popular artists, including Billy Joel, Amy Grant, Elton John, Rod Stewart, Mariah Carey, Wilson Phillips, Paula Abdul and many more. Songs include: Addicted To Love • Baby Baby • Endless Love • Here And Now • Hold On • Lost In Your Eyes • Love Takes Time • Vision Of Love • We Didn't Start The Fire.

00311539 ............................................$14.95

FOR MORE INFORMATION, SEE YOUR LOCAL MUSIC DEALER,
OR WRITE TO:

## HAL•LEONARD™
### CORPORATION
7777 W. BLUEMOUND RD. P.O. BOX 13819 MILWAUKEE, WI 53213

*Prices, contents & availability subject to change without notice.*

0295